Hiraeth

Kayla Bassingthwaite

BookLeaf
Publishing

India | USA | UK

Presentation by *BookLeaf Publishing*

Web: www.bookleafpub.com

E-mail: info@bookleafpub.com

ISBN: 9789357448604

First edition 2022

DEDICATION

To my inner child who didn't know any better;
I'm sorry and I love you.

Dead To My Old Ways

O how indulgence numbed me,
flatlined my feelings free,
pure dopamine released,
a bliss unparalleled.

I cherish the moments before I learned my
behavior was an issue.

The creep of guilt, or the gnawing of shame
didn't come in and dampen the experience yet.
Now that they have, now that I can pinpoint
the red flags and triggers beforehand,
I have not known peace.

Not when my behaviors are so numeric and
trackable--
every purchase on my credit card
pilots me into debt,
the digits on the scale
fluctuate rapidly depending
how well I stayed in control that week.
Someone dispose of the evidence please.

There was still comfort in the toxic routine--
before I cared about my health, my body, my
finances--
before I considered my future at all.

Pleasure is so myopic, yet so
delicious and consuming
to fall into a void of detachment.
Incredulously I considered my behavior
"self-care";
the line of care and destruction is nearly
invisible
when sabotage is so much more erotic.

I can never go back to that state of being;
I've woken up and now I'm dead to my old
ways.

Grace Period

I miss the way I used to love You,
used to trust You,
used to kiss You,
used to seek You,
used to hear You,
used to pray to and praise You,
used to speak of You to anyone who would
listen.

I know You.
I have heard Your voice.
But I don't know my feelings toward You.
I fear You. You feel harsh to me, a disciplinary
father with the belt in his hands.
You draw me back with sweet words that have
changed into sweet nothings--
not because Your intentions have changed, but
because they fall
on welted ears.

This gospel I preach does not reach my heart or
come out of my lips
the same way, and others notice.
An old friend told me she missed the light in my
voice when I would talk about You.

Of course she did;
You are the Light of the world.
Then why do I feel so tumultuous, so tossed
about a cloud-stricken sea
seconds from a tsunami--
the alarms are sounding
but I can't hear them anymore.

I am afraid of Your coming because I'm afraid
You don't love me.
Recover me so I can enter a present where I
love, trust, kiss, seek, hear, pray, praise, and
speak You
deeper than a nostalgia love with opportunity to
misremember.

grief is love with nowhere to go

What do we do when a love proves not to be
fleeting, but long suffering?
When we've grown, healed, evolved, two vines
climbing parallel up the trellis, watching each
other twist and weave but somehow never
trailing too far off?
When I ache for you more now than I did the
first time pen touched the paper
creating words that could never escape my lips,
that stay hidden in ink?
A truth I am afraid you know despite me never
saying so--
but after all this time how could you not?
Is this a mutually agreeable silence--better off
for the both of us, or an exploitation?
I hope this is not just a game to you;
I know our jokes
get out of hand sometimes but do you know
there's always some level of truth in comedy?
I think we both know more than we say
but for now

I'll keep stealing moments with you that are far
more intimate
then I'd care to have with anyone else. I'll listen
to ocean laps
and see with the blue moonlight hue
a person I resent loving
under such unfair circumstances.

Placeholder

A cataclysmic moment for me
Is a beer-tainted blip in your bottle of Scotch.
When I think of how it was everything for me--
Not because of who you are
But because of who I am now because of what
you made me realize--
I feel like I need to brush my teeth
To remove your residue
From my soul.

I ponder what insignificant moments of my story
Were apocalyptic in others.
Or perhaps cringeworthy--
Fond, forgettable, frightening.
Am I a regret or a laugh?

You're the Devil on the mountaintop,
Showing me everything I've ever wanted.
I will always remember you this way,
But I wonder if I was ever worth
A period on a page to you; or
A shit-talk over cigarettes,
A late night ramble,
An eye roll at the sight of me.

Intertwined

How does one forget how you made me feel?
When it's all I can think of?
Now I'm questioning if it was all real
Because you're acting like this love
Never even happened. It wasn't my fault
God tore our souls apart
And our intertwined timeline came to a halt.
The way you blame me is tearing at my heart.
All I've ever wanted was your time,
I never wanted it to be this way.
So please, stop saying I'm fine,
Because I've never been more broken than I am
today.
For all the days you gave your love to me
I sit heartbroken and alone; but now we are free.

Honeybee

It has been so long
Since I heard from you my dear
My heart aches because the one that it will
always belong
is gone and is so far from here.

I want you to be near.
It was you that meant the most to me all along
We are blood, our connection is strong
My sister, our love is forever right and never
wrong.

Listen to my heart's song
That sings in rejoice when you erase my fear
Of being alone, because you prolong
My sadness that in my heart will sear.

But now my heart is clear
Of darkness, and as you peer
Into my broken hearted cheer
You reveal me and make me strong.

It has been so long
Since I heard from you my dear

My heart aches because the one that it will
always belong
is gone and so far from here.

Ocean Codes

Throw the phone in the ocean, stop words from
flowing codes in, deliver a message:
What happened to the voice of my friendships?
Share with me the secret formula for
socializing in a digital age.
Am I getting old, or tired of this
lack of love and communication with
my generation? I can't comprehend
the millennial messages or memes
shared and everyone saying it's the "same"
but you're not all the same. You're special but
I wish you would just say what you wanted
with breath-warmed lips,
not keys that blip so loud
with loneliness. Kiss me full of purpose.

Throw the phone in the ocean,
throw yourself in the ocean,
wash your face with salt, taste the minerals on
your human tongue
and forget that you were ever attached to that
thing.
Let it sink
to the bottom of the reef, step on it
with bold toes, then breathe in air,

fill your lungs with the stuff, and let yourself scream
a scream that Siri can't recognize, can't compute,
"I'm sorry, I didn't quite catch that".
It's okay, let everyone look at you
like you're crazy, at least they're not looking at the screen.
Look at the scream.
The bitter, human scream.

For Things We Can't Undo

Of course I still want to call you my home.
I daydream of building a life with you,
but I'd lose everything and be alone.

I want your kiss to be my days welcome;
the thought alone turns me a bright red hue.
Of course I still want to call you my home.

Every time your name lights up on my phone
I think of all I'd love for us to do,
but I'd lose everything and be alone.

Spiritually, mentally, you have grown
until the person I see is brand new.
Of course I still want to call you my home.

The social consequences are well-known,
to risk it all for things we can't undo,
but I'd lose everything and be alone.

God, you've heard my soul grieving and
moaning
a chance to love without forsaking You.
Of course I still want to call you my home.
But I'd lose everything and be alone

Symptoms

A major symptom
of depression is loss of
interests and passion.

Things I once loved,
hobbies that took me away
from reality.

I binged anime,
a series or two a day;
I love a hero.

I absorbed novels,
voraciously entering
someone else's life.

I wrote hundreds of
short stories, poems; pages of
confessions, fantasy.

I took thousands of
photos on an old Canon
I don't own anymore.

My days were so full
Of activities; eager
for my next project.

My attention span's ruined
by illness wreaking
havoc on this young girl's mind.

Reality is so dull
in the forty hour
work week, all day monotony.

I cancelled Hulu before
finishing a twen-
ty four episode anime.

It takes me months to finish
one book, nevermind
reading entire series.

In college my limited
imagination
became homework, nothing else.

I started painting, but it
takes months to finish
a five by seven canvas.

Depression stolen passion;
self care is detached
from a relentless lifestyle.

20%

It
takes
losing 1/5
of the blood in
your body to go
into shock, to pass
out, to be fatal. My heart
bleeds, recovering from the
shock value of losing you. There's
no way to gauge the damage that's been
done, but it sure feels like I've lost 20% of me
since that day. I'll look for any reason to fixate on
something else; I'll even heal a different hurt to avoid
feeling this one. I'll dig at my scars but God forbid I get
too close to scabs--I'll start bleeding again and I don't know
how many more times I can clot before I hit 20%. The doctors
call me a medical miracle to still stand after losing so much blood.
My body is trying to keep my heart pumping but I've been brain
dead for hours. Someone please pull the plug on me, I was
never meant to be sustained on 80%. Just let my body
die, it'll never be the same. The angels are calling
me with a flatline harmony only I was meant to
hear. I won't be happy until I'm home.

I Can't Tell

Before then, I never felt pain so monstrous
I couldn't feel it at all.
In one fell swoop I lost my two favorite people
and I never got to say goodbye.
Like being consumed in a flame so fast
all of my nerve endings burnt through and I
can't tell
I'm still on fire.

The Scars We Do and Do Not Choose

When I was five years old riding down a hill on
my big wheel
I dragged my inner ankle across the pavement to
slow down
and the imprint has lasted ever since.
I don't even remember it hurting.

When I was twenty years old I crashed my car,
snapping the same ankle nearly 90 degrees,
the bone bursting through my skin.
Oh I definitely remember that hurt.

So when I was 23, for a Valentines Day treat,
I stepped into a tattoo parlor
and above that ankle is a rainbow colored
unicorn.
Needles can bring out such beautiful pigments.

There are scars all over my body
from the life I've lived, my mistakes and my
joys--

how beautiful that though
we didn't choose some of these imperfections
there are those we can.
We choose to sit through hours of pain
to come out new--I'll die a patchwork
of flowers and moons and white lines and jagged
pink gashes
and who knows what else--but please remember
in a life of chosen pain we still maintain a
semblance of control.

Disappeared

I grieve for the people I thought
I would see you become,
written over by the last memories I didn't know
I'd have of you.
I wish they were better ones.
I wish I didn't have to pretend you never existed.
I wish I could explain to you that I didn't know
you'd be growing up without me.
I wish we never got close so you wouldn't be
hurt by losing me.

I was supposed to see your first day of school.
We were going to go to the park,
the aquarium,
the beach,
the library,
everything new and exciting, all for you.
I would slide down the slide with you one
hundred more times,
watch Frozen every night in my bed just to hear
your tiny voice say,
"I love you".

I've spent so much time pretending you weren't
important to me

I forgot how horrible it must be that I was
important to you.
I can't imagine how confused you must be
knowing you're not
allowed to love me anymore.
I'm so sorry for every time you think of me.
I'm so sorry for every moment you feel the way
I do right now.
I'm sorry the memory of me is imprinted on so
many parts of your life.
I hope you truly like being there more than you
liked being with me,
and it makes this hurt less for you.

I read it takes toddlers approximately six months
to forget a person;
please please forget me quickly,
make better memories to replace ours.

Were

We pronounce the "were" in werewolf like
"wear",
as in a human wearing creature skin--
a DNA fur coat, a conditional metamorphosis
cloaked in night with the opportunity to ravage.
Entertaining a nature not free to express.

Or we could pronounce it "where"--
like where do you hold your tongue in your
mouth
while hiding your secrets? Where do you run to
alone by the moonlight guiding your beastly
footsteps?

But stand alone we pronounce it "were", the past
tense of "are";
like the version of yourself you cling to.
Remember before you were the wolf…
My loved ones fondly say;
I wish I could forget this was who
you all preferred.
And who I wish I still was when I wake up"
The person your loved ones
fondly say "remember before you were the
wolf…"

and I could forget this was who you all
preferred.
And who I wish I still was when I wake up
and my skin doesn't fit right on my body
anymore.

Pruning

Resurrection always comes after death.
The vampire, zombie, phoenix, and Christ
rising from coffins, virus, ashes, and Hades.
Spring never fails to arrive no matter the winter
preceding.
365 days ago I was slipping away in
self-induced sleep, swallowing
an unconsciousness I intended to be permanent.
It wasn't.
I wish I could hold myself and beg her to be
okay--I know nothing would change.

I grieve for a 2020 girl who saw no way out,
whose despair clouded every beautiful thing
surrounding her.
Yet, I tried to end it over far less than the pain
I've bore into the eyes of since.
I have far more to lament than to rejoice in.
I bereaved deeper, healed deeper;
I can't say I always coped well,
but coping implies the intention
to stay. I'll cope a thousand times poorly
if it means I keep doing it at all.

I look back on my past self with a love and
compassion I still can't show
My present self.
"You tried so hard to survive all that pain
unpacked.
You were so young. You didn't know."
That doesn't mean I know any better now,
though I should.
Maybe I never will.
I'm so so sorry, my dear, that this chasm was too
deep to cross. I have put everything
into healing us so we never fall into it
or crave its dark embrace so badly we jump.

The void calls my name in a dog whistle pitch,
the distance
unsure but changing in volume like a steam train
echoing its horn across the entire canyon--
is it around the corner, or miles off?
Either way, I'm still laying horizontal across the
tracks
with no energy to move.
Still, I think I can outrun it this time. I'm not
convinced,
but I've had a whole year to train.

I don't know if I'm happy I lived or not.
I pruned so many people, so many bad habits;
I pruned the dreams I had for me and for us.

I've pruned so much I don't know what I'm left
with other than thorns.
My leaves that stretched closest to the Sun
have all burned away by now--but
my roots are thick enough to withstand
the whacker, the weather,
the worms and the waste.

Shifting

It is more probable to believe than not
that multiple realities exist when every choice
has led me to this one--
every decision made by me
and those with power over me has snowballed
into who I am, and who I subconsciously have
no choice
to become this late in my life.

If a butterfly wing can be a catalyst for chaos,
disrupting whole realities creating continuum
shifts,
think of all the leaves misplaced, a caterpillar
in the wind, a tremor in the Earth
that could cause another branch in the vine;
O the webs of time we weave with all our
mistakes.

How moldable are our lives in a lifetime of
mostly monotony?
What footsteps are butterfly wings and what are
ordained?
Maybe the theory only fascinates me because of
the craving

for control over my own little reality, and that it
was me
who created this world for myself,
regardless of the damage, the power,
the hand others had over me.
And I can still change that undoubtedly,
Not you, or all of you before you--
me.

Think of the realities we don't even exist in,
how the circumstances of our existence are
contingent
on a predetermined choice by a human, or a
God,
or the pull of the tide, or cosmic happenstance--
our reality shaped before we have the chance
to alter it, and then we spend our whole lives
influencing it by our own undoings.
Who really controls the timeline?

I wonder if there is a prevailing thread of reality,
the Destiny Strand, The Way Things Are
Supposed to Be,
the Ultimate Timeline wrangled and designed.

In what timelines do we know which god?
In which timeline do we assign responsibility,
and to who?

In which timeline do we need a Savior, and how
many do I kneel before Him?
I am unsure if I prefer this one where I do,
or one where we did not need such a One at all.
One with the garden still intact,
peace reigning my days alongside the Creator;
someone not needed
but benevolent enough
to ignore the creatures whispering
doubts from the creation.
Maybe you could give all of humanity the same
choice
and we'd never choose Him.
No prevailing timeline, just a predictable species
always failing ourselves in the same way
despite the lessons we've learned in every
thread.
How easy to then design
a timeline for humans
so predicated on every step--
a species
with no surprises.

A Summoning Trill

Summertime was never blue to
the Child's Mind--tons to do and
all the freedom to do it too.

Summertime had its own tune--
a summoning Trill, the promise
of popsicles consumed too soon.

Always a new land to explore--
Imagination building worlds
for conquering before morning.

The days passed slower in summer.
At least I think they were--they can't
have been as fast as the hours now.

Breaks stopped
after student
status ceased, working straight through
from June-August; nothing to sever
the relentless tasks piling on.
Responsibilities
are all I know
lately.

I hear my mother's voice yelling again--
the air conditioning, skyrocketing
electric bills; now I'm understanding
how little money stretched after you gain
forty hours worth of it. The slight pain
of half of your bills accumulating.
But at least the cold is so comforting
I almost forget the bank account strain.

Years ago, summer glittered like jasper;
I remember racing home when streetlights
flick on. Bike rides, freedom, and pure laughter.
There are days I never see the sunlight,
clocking in before and leaving after
the days had passed into hot, lonely nights.

Resumes and Cover Letters

What else can I do to prove to you I'm worth the
chance?
I've been employed every day since age 17,
I have a whole four year degree proving I can
read and write,
I've been nominated for awards, certifying that
when I say I'm proficient in something
I mean it.
I am a jack of all trades
and became a master of all--
imagine the energy I could bring to the career
I actually care about. My devotion
damn near religious
for you. Just let me prove it.
I'll turn your words into gold like every other
position I've touched, please watch me.

What is it about my person that makes you
forget
how attractive I am on paper?
Am I not as carefully crafted as my cover letter?
I can't be shy or anxious on a manuscript.

How many interview workshops can I attend,
how many mock questionnaires can I take
to prepare myself to not be good enough for you
again?

I've always been far too ahead of myself,
but I envision myself in all of your cubicles,
the miles in my car ticking higher from driving
to your office.
I consider the projects I could be managing;
the conversations I would have with my support
system all about how I'm finally doing
what I've always wanted.
Knowing that He finally wanted for me what
I've wanted all along
and I would revel in a long awaited blessing.
So when I get rejected from another opportunity
I'm not just disappointed; I'm watching my
future reality crumble.
All that could have been but never will be
slips from my grasp and all I have left
is this fucking email.

Hero's Journey

Walk through the threshold of your past home
after being away, exercising your new
independence
and know in that span of time since
you have changed.

Your own mind doesn't see the art on the walls
or the furniture the same --
it sees new stains in the carpet
and the clutter piling in your old room.
You've adventured and experienced and grown
more than little you would imagine,
but after you didn't come into this room
to process it.
The bed you slept in
didn't absorb this part of your history--
the wooden floors don't record the footsteps
of all your secrets anymore.
The pages in your book are missing from this
library,
 They don't own the rights to it anymore--
you're under a new contract.

You've gone on a hero's journey since you left;
You're not returning to the same home--

the mold no longer fits you, you'll crack the
edges of everything you've become
if you try.

Skincells

How
sweet that
in seven
years I will have
a body never
touched by your ill-intentioned fingertips.

Envisioning a future I've healed in,
peace envelops me,
and I almost
think I can
forgive
you.

www.ingramcontent.com/pod-product-compliance
Lightning Source LLC
Chambersburg PA
CBHW070613160726
48003CB00005B/2247